THE CARE LINE

PIPPA HAWKINS

Published by Cinnamon Press
Meirion House
Tanygrisiau
Blaenau Ffestiniog
Gwynedd, LL41 3SU
www.cinnamonpress.com

The right of Pippa Hawkins to be identified as author of this work has been asserted by her in accordance with the Copyright, Designs and Patent Act, 1988. Copyright © 2018 Pippa Hawkins.
ISBN: 978-1-78864-000-8

British Library Cataloguing in Publication Data. A CIP record for this book can be obtained from the British Library.

All rights reserved. No part of this publication may be reproduced, stored in a retrieval system, or transmitted in any form or by any means, electronic, mechanical, photocopying, recording or otherwise without the prior written permission of the publishers. This book may not be lent, hired out, resold or otherwise disposed of by way of trade in any form of binding or cover other than that in which it is published, without the prior consent of the publishers.

Designed and typeset in Palatino by Cinnamon Press. Cover design by Jan Fortune. Printed in Poland

Cinnamon Press is represented in the UK by Inpress Ltd and in Wales by the Welsh Books Council

Acknowledgements

I would like to thank Julie-ann Rowell for her guidance in editing these poems. Thanks also to my fellow poets in Bristol groups who listened and offered suggestions for improvements. Thanks to my family and friends who have encouraged me to write and to Jan Fortune for her support through the publication process.

Contents

The Dossette Boxes	7
The Struggle to See	8
The Joys of Parkinson's	9
Your Suitcase	10
The Care Line	11
September 17th 2014	12
Anxiety	14
What the Doctor Ordered	16
Two Carers Meet	17
Dementia Museum	18
Toxic Delirium Summer	20
After The Fall	21

For carers everywhere and also for Andrew

The Care Line

The Dosette Boxes

My hands once spread
butter and marmite onto
wholemeal bread, sliced fruit,
to pack in boxes for our sons.

Now, with veins bulging they
grapple with white, brown, pink ovals.
I count them into seven boxes.
Seven doses a day for seven days.

Pink replaces lost brain cells,
a white one slows your bladder,
the brown one speeds your bowels.

I clip the lids shut, set them
in order beside your bed. Later
I see your hands fumble to release
your three hourly taste of hope.

The names are constellations
that travel with you through the dome of day:

Stelevo, Entacapone,

Clopidogral, Madopar.

The Struggle to See

Your glasses are on the sideboard.
Walking stick taps its way from bedroom to kitchen.
The route is a cul-de-sac, just past the table you collide

with the dog, turn and make your way around
the chair, breakfast encrusted on your chin,
but your glasses are still on the sideboard.

You pick up the newspaper to start the crossword
but cannot see the clues. I suppress a smile,
The Guardian is a cul-de-sac of pages that will not fold.

You squint and hold one page towards
the light. I am tempted to intervene
because your glasses are still on the sideboard.

The dog sniffs the glasses as if to guide
you to them. But neither of us can suceed
because your brain is a cul-de-sac. You cannot decide

how best to reproduce what was a well-tried
pattern of action and reaction. To walk the line
that will lead you to glasses still waiting on the sideboard,
help you round the cul-de-sac of hazards that fills the kitchen.

The Joys of Parkinson's

Every morning I try not to shout
but it doesn't usually work.
It could be the stench of urine on a chair that sets
me off, or a flicker of anger on your face.

It doesn't always work
my desire to stay calm.
It could be a flicker of anger on your face,
or perhaps you have forgotten to take your pills.

My desire to stay calm
evaporates before breakfast.
Perhaps you have forgotten to take your pills
and I cannot move you.

Most days it disappears before breakfast,
my wish to recreate myself.
I cannot move you,
you do not understand me.

My wish to recreate myself
seems as difficult as birthing a new universe.
You cannot hear beyond the shouting,
because your brain cells are dying.

You cannot understand me
because your brain cells are dying.
Each morning I decide not to shout,
but most days my decision vapourises before breakfast.

Your Suitcase

You know that silver coloured one I bought in Jolly's.
You kept it locked on top of the wardrobe
hoping for a ticket to Crete or Paris.

Then one day the first clasp shot
open—I got a hint of what was inside.
The slab of Anchor butter that had migrated
to the top rack of the dishwasher,

reading glasses you had moved to chill
in the fridge. Your in-tray overflowing with old
sweet wrappers and broken pens.

One Sunday afternoon the lid lifted,
revealed a hoard of mobile
phones all set to call 999.
Climbing up the sides towards the lip

were the car keys you lost two months ago,
followed by a procession
of spent bank cards cut into squares.

The wrinkled poly-pocket at the bottom
was full of names you had struggled
to remember. Your best friend Graham,
our grandson Seth.

I tried to collect the debris, stuff it back,
sit on the lid, click the locks,
but it glared at me, rattled its resistance.

The Care Line

Just as a ship has a line
that marks
how far it can sink
beneath the water

so my caring for you
has an unseen line;
if I cross it
I may
drown.

September 17th 2014

Early call.
Carer cancels.
Her car stuttered
to a stop in Bishop Sutton.

I crawl out of bed.
Wake you up,
help you shower.
Usual struggle with the towel.

I kneel, reluctant servant, at your feet,
connect the incontinence tube,
pants, trousers
twisted, uncomfortable.

Downstairs, my tears fall into
porridge. After breakfast,
sweaty hands smear
the steering wheel as we drive

to your singing group.
Your accompaniment
slightly offbeat. You are
unaware of the deluge

of panic washing over me.
To the surgery for
a flu injection.
I try to enjoy the sun

but feel like the bird
who flew into my shed last week,
threw itself against windows,
desperate to find a way out.

I ring your social worker.
Can hardly speak, just words, sobs.
You cannot understand,
neither can I.

She comes. Calls her office.
I catch a few words.
Carer breakdown. Respite bed.
Emergency funding.

Mystified, you move out
with your half-packed
silver suitcase.

Anxiety

Something is in my bed.
I look inside, flinch as I see
the swirling gravity of a
black hole

chaos of non-being. My thoughts bounce
off its
event horizon.
My brain can't
process them. They fly

into space,
join the
rings of Saturn
causing ripples,
agitated bumps
in once beautiful dust-clouds.

Then there are insistent thoughts
that bombard my brain from
distant galaxies,
like the asteroids that rain

down on earth in August,
but there's no
light-show just
sweaty hands,
a stomach that never stops
digesting.

I try deflecting them, but they gather
in groups,
get caught in Jupiter's
winds, accelerate until I hear
a tiny note

emerge from the storm,
it swells into a
single syllable—
help.

What the Doctor Ordered

As an antidote to grief the doctor
says, *Take these.* Hands me white
pills, capsules yellow

as the sun. At first—euphoria.
I am calm as a tranquilliser,
but biting at my heels are

withdrawls. I become a rabbit
caught in headlights. Each
decrease hits back with punch

after punch of panic. The restless
sleep of the addict. In my battle
against milligrams I search for

counter-attack. Try rearguard
action, slow my breathing, take
deep gulps of life.

Withdrawal drags on,
an oversized advent
calendar. Windows open

show their wares. Behind some,
a scattering of stars, stunning
seascapes. Others are wild sea-storms.

But there are no wise men, no caskets
of myrrh—the last depicts unending
mountain ranges which I must climb.

Two Carers Meet

I am in hospital, temperature stratospheric,
pneumonia locked in lungs.
Sometimes I glimpse him through

half closed eyes,
watch him stroking her hair,
massaging her feet.

He seems so devoted,
so gentle, she lies still,
silent, oxygen tubes strapped to her nose.

I turn away,
guilty, jealous. I knew that while
I cared for you, I was far from perfect.

Plonked food on the table,
wanted to hide in sleep,
to run away, to scream.

The next day, I meet him in the corridor.
He tells me of her alcohol abuse,
of stopping work to care for her.

I talk too, about Parkinsons's Disease,
dementia, exhaustion. It is short, our talk,
but our eyes meet, briefly.

Later he comes to my bed,
asks if I want anything at the shop.
I say a pear would be good.

Much later I find a fruit bowl
by my bed, overflowing
with grapes, bananas, apples and pears.

Dementia Museum

The charge for entry is my rapid breathing,
sore eyes, tight shoulders, muscles braced.

The entrance hall is filled with colourful mobiles
of your lost bank cards. One wall covered

in your pin numbers printed on fine tissue
paper. In the first recess, a glass dome

contains a set of car keys you will never use again.
On the far wall, repeating slides show brain scans

with expanding rivers of dark tissue flowing
towards each other, that join to make a delta

of emptiness. In the centre of the room an abstract
sculpture created with your broken CD cases and paper-

inserts showing details of a Beethoven symphony, Chopin
nocturnes, medieval choruses. A set of images decorate

one wall: your birth certificate, us outside the church,
smiling, confirmation of your degree in Theology.

The last image, your RICE dementia score.
The smell of stale urine welcomes me

to your Dementia Bed. Brown stains on the bottom
sheet, bright yellow on your duvet.

Pyjamas crumpled, soiled, scattered
across the floor. Two used incontinence pads draped

on the bedside table. I take a break, fill a few tissues,
try some deep breathing before I visit the final exhibit.

A photographic time machine displays your face
from boyhood to the first signs of illness:

expressionless eyes, confused smile. The sound-
system pumps out recordings of your bass voice,

stomach churning harmonies in perfect pitch. A skill
held safe in some unidentified region of your brain.

Toxic Delirium Summer

Dreaming of escape, I pack the car: tent, bed, camping stove, dog.
Pitch near Skomer, gannets diving, boots ringing on cliff paths.
Just before the second sunset your nursing home message me
through ether: emergency doctor, ambulance, hospital.

Night was drizzly, wet. Sleepless, I wait till gulls
call me at sunrise. Mud-encrusted trousers,
dripping tent. I pass Haverfordwest, St Clear's, Swansea,
thinking I might miss your last breath.

I find you in Zone D, still breathing, surrounded by drips,
talking of space ships, aliens. Nurses desperate to know
your history quiz me. But not regarding mountains climbed, tents
pitched, coast paths walked,
their concern is about what you have become.

He can walk with a stick.
Get out of a chair. Feed himself.

In between ward rounds I long for my tent,
musty dampness,freedom. When delerium retreats,
you return to your own bed.
I dry my tent, drink in the necter of its canvas.

After the Fall

Eyes shut. Black. Someone
opens them, I blink in the light,
then nothing but pain.
Sometimes I feel her here,
a cold cup on my lips.
I drink, it's good.
Then a warm spoon,
my mouth opens like a fledgling,
I swallow.

A slit of light.
Black shapes on the ceiling,
string on the bed, tickling my
hands. Try to shake it off.
What is this place,
this bed? I feel a pill
on my tongue,
sharp knives down
my leg. Pain.

I am wet, then dry.
Hands hurt under my back.
I feel sick, my head
throbs. It's just me
with the shapes.
She's not here.
Light then dark ,
the sharp blades of pain.
I used to walk, there's
my stick but black shapes
cover it. Shadows come, prick
my arm, more pain, blood, bruises.
She is here, the glass,
the spoon. I think I know her,
say her name.
She asks mine.
I say *Andrew*.